Whom God Hath Joined Together

Contents

Fred Bock Music Company

Whither Thou Goest

Ruth 1: 16, and
RICHARD A. DEWEY

Music by
RICHARD A. DEWEY

Whith - er thou go - est, I will go.

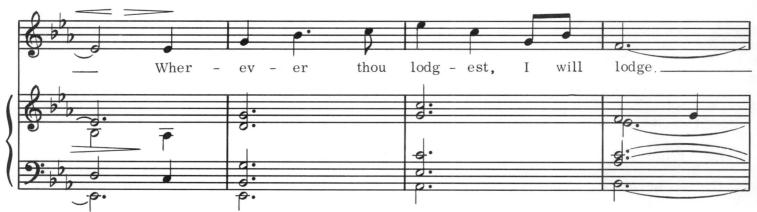

Wher - ev - er thou lodg - est, I will lodge.

Thy peo - ple shall be my peo - ple, my

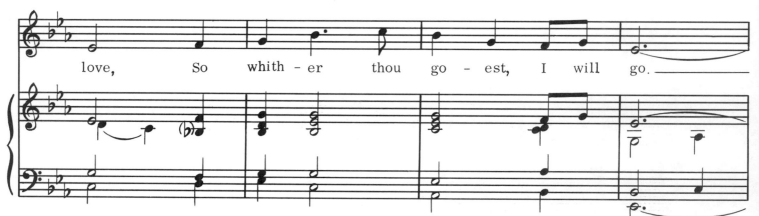

love, So whith - er thou go - est, I will go.

To thee all my love___ I be - stow.____

As one, shall the two of us grow.____

Thy peo - ple shall be my peo - ple, my

love. So whith - er thou go - est, I will go.____

rit.

Let Us Climb the Hill Together

Words and Music by
PAUL CLARK

Moderately

I _____ have wait-ed such a long, long_ time_____ for this day_ to come;

And _____ all I have to give is the love from God's on-ly son_____ He

gave to me to give_____ un-to you. I

pray_____ that God will be with us night_and day,_ guide us all_ the way in our

life. There will be no strife with Je - sus Christ_and His King - dom which has

come_ and made it pos-si-ble_____ for you and I_ to be one._____

I will make you queen_ of my home,_ un-der the glo-ry of the King.

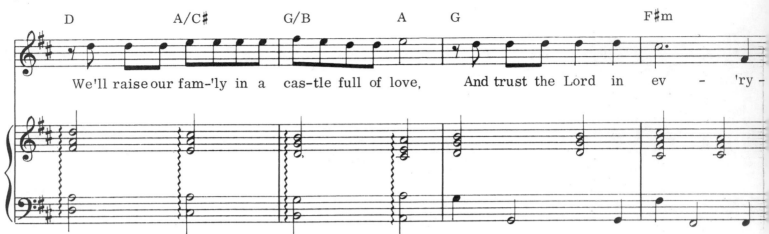

We'll raise our fam-'ly in a cas-tle full of love, And trust the Lord in ev - 'ry -

thing, _____ Let us sing _____ to the King Hal - le - le - jah! _____ In

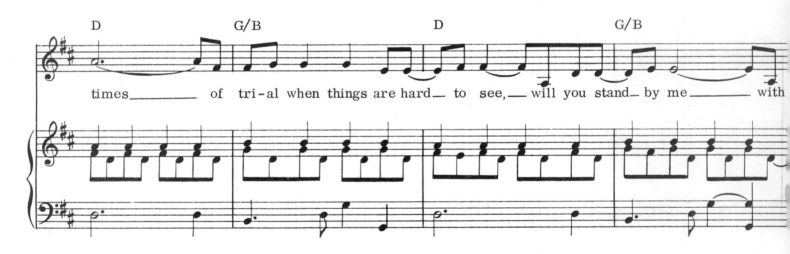

times _____ of tri - al when things are hard _ to see, _ will you stand _ by me _____ with

love? It can heal the pain, so let _____ it rain on the roof of my

soul._____ There is no hole_____ that__love can't fill,_____ So

let us climb, let us climb the hill to-geth-

-er,__ let us climb the hill to-geth-er,__ let us climb_____ the hill_____ to-

geth-er,__ let us climb the hill to-geth-er._____

Wedding Song

Arr. by PAUL JOHNSON
Moderato

Words and Music by
GARY HALLQUIST

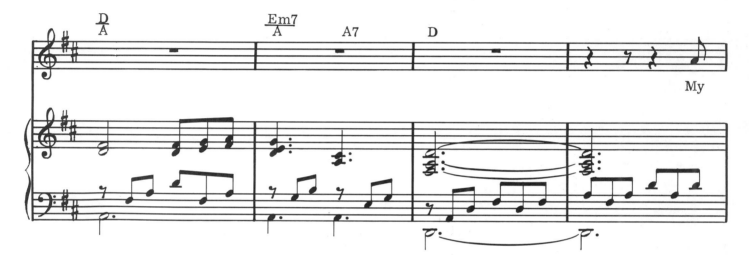

son (love) _____ at-tend to my words. _____ In-
love, _____ my life ___ is Yours. _____ To

cline _____ your ear to my say - ings. _____ Let them
have _____ for - ev - er to cher - ish. ___ In

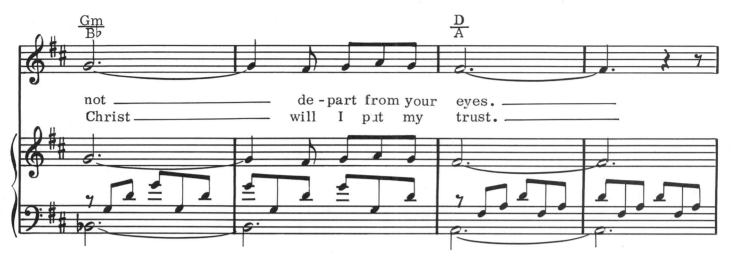

not _____ de - part from your eyes. _____
Christ _____ will I put my trust. _____

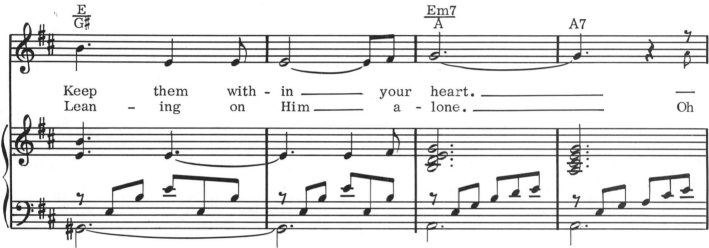

Keep them with - in _____ your heart. _____ __ Oh
Lean - ing on Him _____ a - lone. _____

Go _____ in - to all the world. _____ And pro -
Lord, _____ with Christ in our hearts. _____ _ We

claim _____ the ris - en Sa - vior. _____
bow _____ _ hum-bly be - fore _____ You. With the

Go _____ for I will be with You. ____ We
love _____ You gave on the cross _____

E - ven un - til _____ the end. _____
vow _____ to live Your life a - new. _____

CHORUS

I will go _____

For where you go I will go. _____

And where you lodge, I will lodge. _____ Your

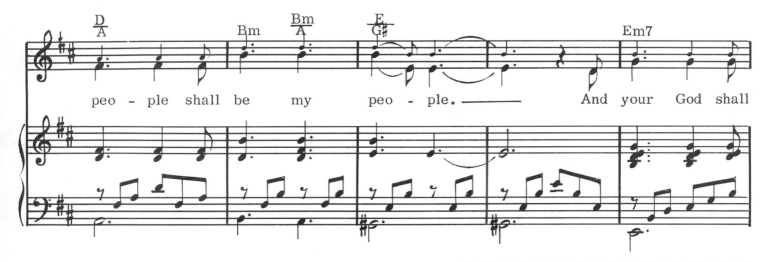

peo - ple shall be my peo - ple. _____ And your God shall

be my God. _____

2. My your God shall be my God. _____ And

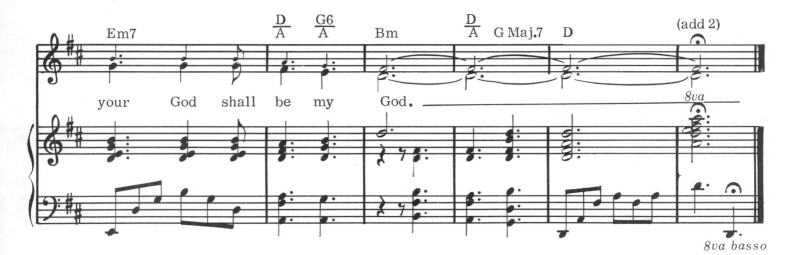

your God shall be my God. _____

8va basso

Fanfare and Processional

(Sw.) full organ without reeds
without 16'

[Gt.] full organ with reeds
sw. to gt.

Ped: sw. to ped., bourdon 16' 8',

(A#) 03 7647 335 No Vibrato

[A#] 21 7857 456 No Vibrato

[B] 32 7868 568

Ped: 55

Music by
FRED BOCK

I. Fanfare

II. Processional

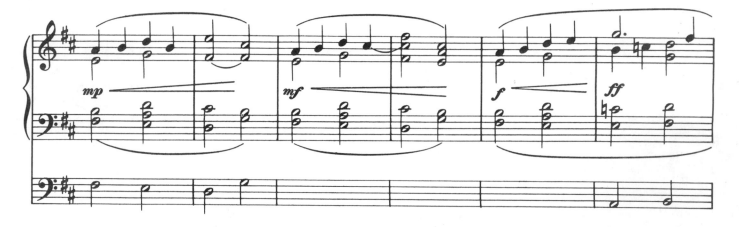

Final Ending

B Add
fff (sfz)

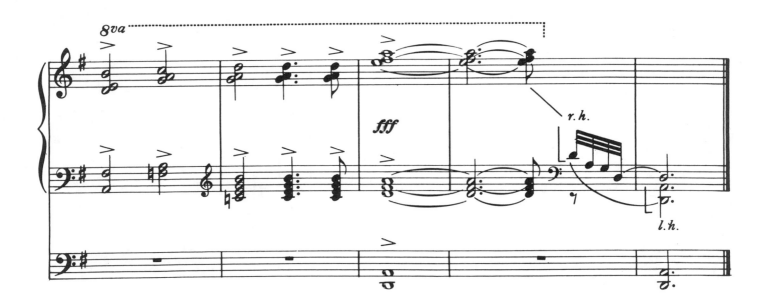

8va

fff

r.h.

l.h.

Recessional

Sw. full flute chorus
and diapasons, without 16'

Gt. full organ, sw. to gt.

Ped: sw. to ped., diapasons 16', 8'

G#   No Vibrato
A# 21 7857 456 No Vibrato
B   32 7868 568

Ped: 54

Music by
RALPH CARMICHAEL

Brightly and joyfully

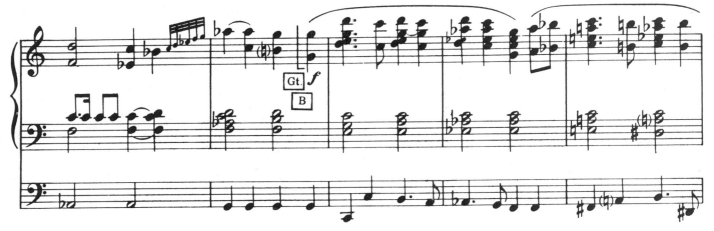

O Perfect Love

Words by
DOROTHY GURNEY
and FRED BOCK

Music by
FRED BOCK

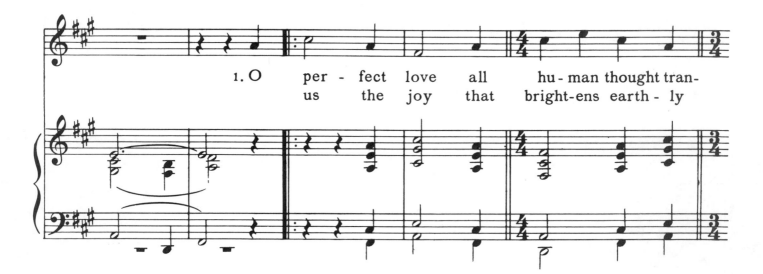

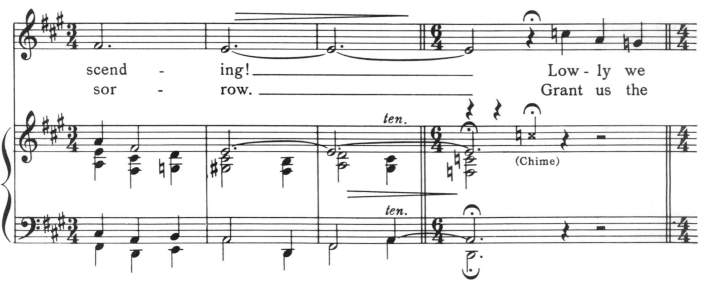

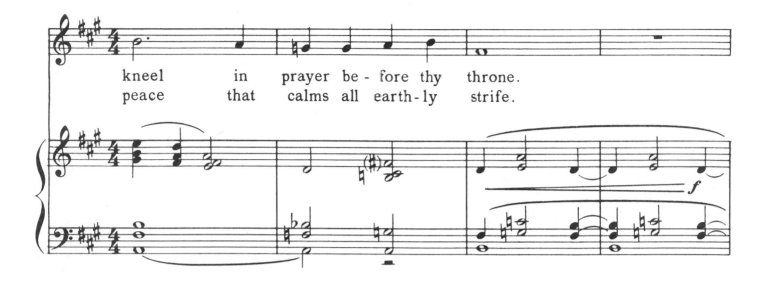

kneel in prayer be - fore thy throne.
peace that calms all earth-ly strife.

That ours may be _____ the
Grant that our lives _____ through

(Sw.)

(Chime)

love that knows no end - ing _____ Whom thou for -
God's own grace and pow - er _____ Will show His

2nd time no breath

ev - er - more dost join in one_____
love, will

2. Grant

show His love through

us._____

Tell Me With Thine Eyes

Words and Music by
GORDON YOUNG

1. O   tell   me   with   thine   eyes   that   love   is
2. Or   leave   me   with   a   to -   ken   of   thy

all   for   aye,   and   I   will
love,   true   heart,   and   I   will

give   thee   a   sign. _____
send _____   thee   mine. _____

O, sa - cred hour of joy, with us re - main,

I will not ev - er go from thee a - gain, from thee a -

gain. O love, tell me, O tell me with thine

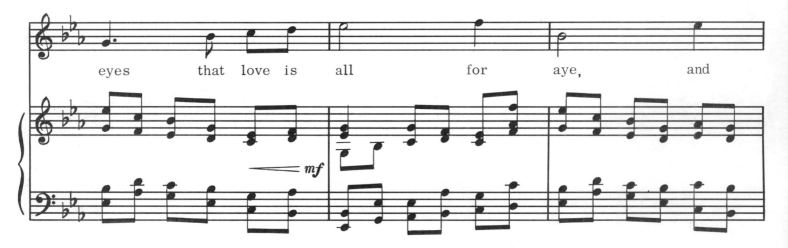

eyes that love is all for aye, and

is ___ for - ev - er di - vine. ___

Or leave me with a to - ken of thy love, dear

heart, and I will give ___ thee

mine. ___

When Adam Was Created

Text adapted by
Erna Moorman

Traditional
Arr. by Fred Bock

Moderato, with expression

(Flute 8')
mp
Organ or Piano

1. When

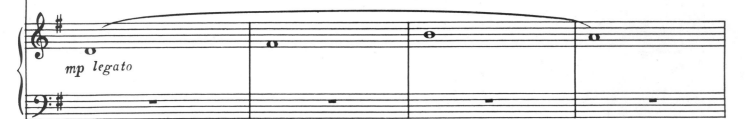

Ad - am was cre - a - ted, He dwelt in E - den's shade   As

mp legato

Mo - ses has re - lat - ed, be - fore his bride God made.   Ten

thou-sand times ten thou - sand of crea-tures swarmed a - round,   Be -

3. This wom-an was not tak - en from Ad-am's head you know, That she must not rule o - ver him is ev - i-dent-ly so. This wom-an was not tak - en from Ad-am's feet you see, And he must love and care for her the mean-ing seems to be.

(no pedal)

(Add pedal)

mf ©*a little faster*

4. This wom-an, she was

tak - en from un-der Ad - am's arm, And she must be pro-tect - ed from

hun-ger and from harm. This wom-an, she was tak - en from near to Ad-am's

heart. By this we are di - rect - ed that they must nev - er

part. 5. To you, most lov-ing bride - groom, to you, most lov-ing

bride, Be sure you live the good life, and for your house pro-

vide; To bring each oth-er pleas - ure through your en-tire____

life.____ This is the hap-py du - ty of ev-'ry man and wife.

(Full organ)

(Strings 8'-4'-2')

(Add pedal)

* Organ play one octave higher.

God Has Given You to Me

Arr. by Kennard Mc Nichols

Words and Music by
BRYAN JEFFERY LEECH

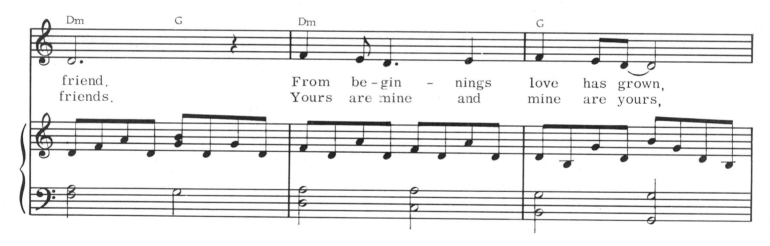

1. God has giv-en you to me ___ as my lov-ing
2. God is join-ing, here to-day, ___ fam-i-lies and

friend. From be-gin-nings love has grown,
friends. Yours are mine and mine are yours,

may its grow-ing nev-er end. ___ From be-gin-nings
how the rich-ness blends! ___ Yours are mine and

mine to you, to have and hold. 4. You are love-ly
6. We shall on-ly

in my eyes,— I wor-ship and a - dore.
be ful-filled _____ as we're filled with Him.

But my heart de - ter - mines this, I must love God
God a-lone can light our love when the flame grows

more. _____ Though I love you oh so well,
dim. _____ For God is light and God is love,

I must love God more. _____
when the flame grows dim. _____
5. I love you
7. Our love may

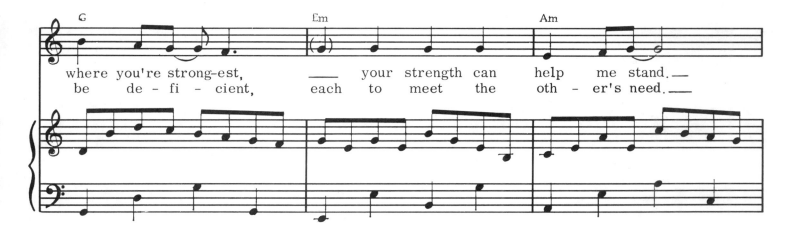

where you're strong-est, _____ your strength can help me stand. _____
be de - fi - cient, each to meet the oth - er's need. _____

_____ I love you where you're weak - est. _____ There I'll care, I'll
We must bor - row from God's plen - ty for God is love! Yes,

help you there, and give your heart a help -ing hand.
God is love! Yes God is love, is

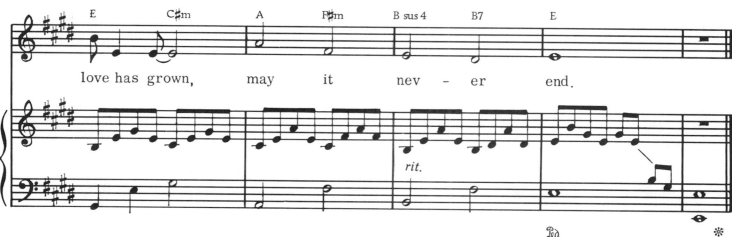

The Greatest of These is Love

Words by
ANNE DICKAU

Music by
DAVID DICKAU

As long as the Son sur-rounds us with His love,_____ we will be as one.__

For with love we'll grow and share and learn____

and be for - ev - er.

mf For

love nev - er fail - eth and love nev-er dies.

but it grows as we give.____

There are but three things that re - main:____ faith, hope, and

Take our fu-ture and take our dreams and use them for Your will. For

love, Your love.

Bless us with Your love.

The Lord's Prayer

Text from
The Scriptures

Inez McCune Williamson

Our Fath - er, which art in Heav - en,_____ Hal - low - ed be Thy

Name, Hal - low - ed be Thy Name.____ Thy King - dom

come, Thy will be done, in earth, as it is in

Heav - en, in earth, as it is in Heav - en. _____

Give us this day our dai - ly bread, and for-give us our debts, as we for-give our

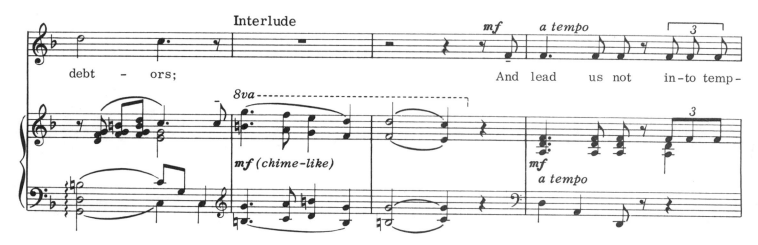

Interlude

debt - ors; And lead us not in-to temp-

ta - tion, but de - liv - er us frcm e - vil, For Thine is the

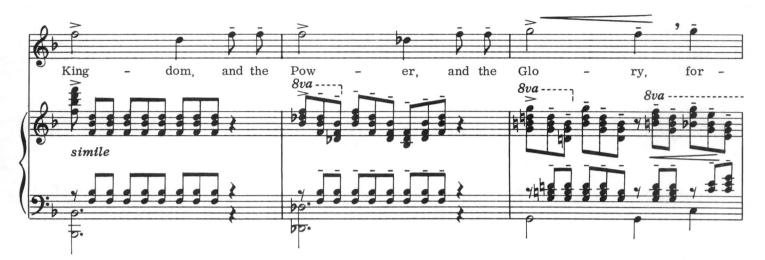

King - dom, and the Pow - er, and the Glo - ry, for -

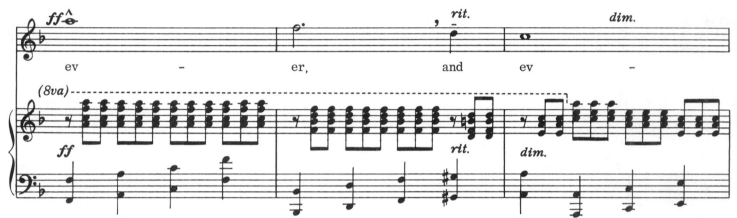

ev - er, and ev -

er, A - men,

A - men, A - men.

Can Two Walk Together

Arr. by Roland Tabell

Words and Music by
BRYAN JEFFERY LEECH

1. Can two walk to-geth-er, ex-cept they let God lead them? Can two walk to-geth-er ex-cept He guide their way? Can there be u-ni-ty?

(2. Can) two walk to-geth-er, with-out the Lord to guide them, Who sees the dark-est fu-ture as if that dark were day? For He, and He a-lone,

The Love That Lasts A Lifetime

Arr. by David R. Talbott

Words and Music by
BRYAN JEFFERY LEECH

1. The love that lasts a life-time is a love that grows and
(2. The) love of man and wo-man is a flame each must pro-

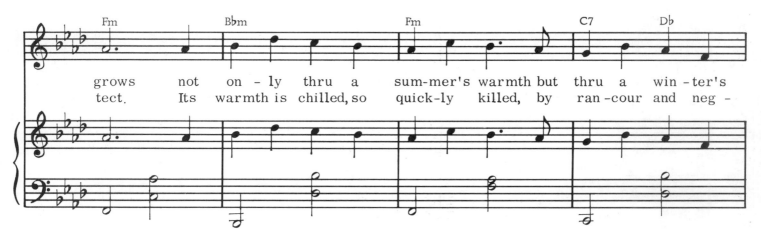

grows not on-ly thru a sum-mer's warmth but thru a win-ter's
tect. Its warmth is chilled, so quick-ly killed, by ran-cour and neg-

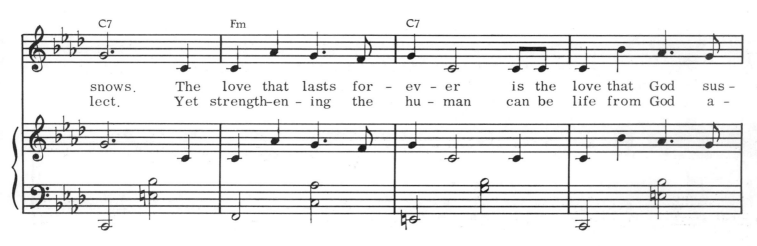

snows. The love that lasts for-ev-er is the love that God sus-
lect. Yet strength-en-ing the hu-man can be life from God a-

tains which still may thrive and come a-live when youth no more re-
bove to bring to birth in homes on earth His faith-ful-ness and

rubato

mains. Love like this is can-did, love like this is
love. Love like this is al-ways slow-est to con-

kind: Al-ways keeps the oth - er per-son's good in mind. Love like this is nev-er
demn: Love like this, the source from which all vir-tues stem. Love like this is just a

rough and nev-er rude, ___ Love like this can nev-er, ev-er be sub-
faint re-flec-tion of ___ all that's found with-in the Fa-ther's ho-ly

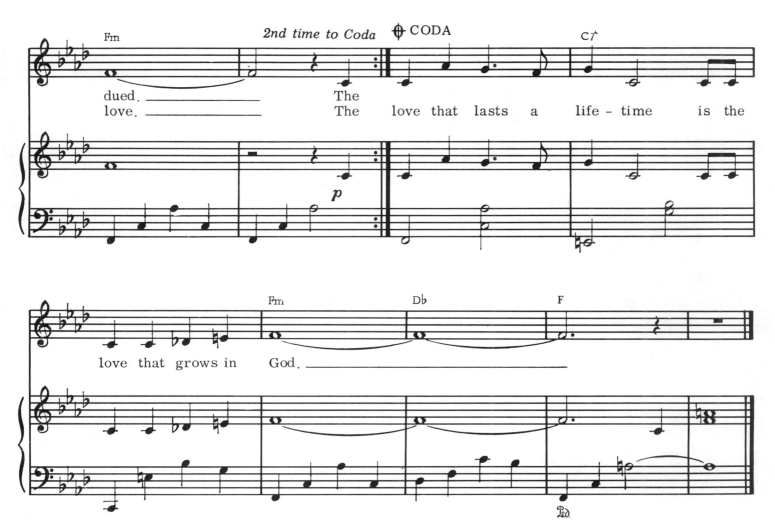

dued. _____ The

love. _____ The love that lasts a life-time is the

love that grows in God. _____

Whom God Hath Joined Together

. . . . *let no man put asunder.*